APPOINTMENT WITH GOD

Some other books in this series

Full list on application to:
25–35 City Road, London, E.C.1.

APPOINTMENT WITH GOD

*Some Thoughts on
Holy Communion*

J. B. PHILLIPS

WYVERN BOOKS

PUBLISHED BY
THE EPWORTH PRESS
(FRANK H. CUMBERS)
25–35 CITY ROAD, LONDON, E.C.1

First published in 1954
First issued in Wyvern Books in 1962

PRINTED AND BOUND IN ENGLAND BY
HAZELL WATSON AND VINEY LTD
AYLESBURY AND SLOUGH

AUTHOR'S NOTE

The addresses printed here are a reproduction, with little alteration, of a series of Lenten Addresses given to the people of my church at St. John's, Redhill, Surrey. It is obvious that the huge, mysterious, as well as controversial, subject of Holy Communion could not be covered in twenty little books such as this. The intention is not in any way to cover the subject but to help the ordinary Communicant to a more intelligent and satisfying approach to this central Christian rite.

In the nature of the case it is written from the standpoint of an Anglican Vicar, but it is certainly not written in any exclusive spirit. Where it attacks what the author believes to be erroneous teaching in Roman Catholic or Anglo-Catholic circles, there is certainly no intention of attacking fellow-Christians themselves. But it would be dishonest and cowardly to avoid altogether the controversial. A man can only set down what he sincerely believes to be true; but he must not be so bigoted as to suppose that other points of view may not be just as sincerely held by fellow-Christians of different schools of thought.

Redhill 1954   J. B. P.

CONTENTS

PREFACE

'I WISH to goodness Sister wouldn't go to early Service on the third Sunday,' remarked one young nurse to another. 'She always comes back in such a filthy temper.' That perfectly genuine remark is used here, not uncharitably, but simply to illustrate the foolishness of 'going to Communion' merely out of a sense of duty. If we are not refreshed and strengthened, if we do not really receive something of Christ which will make our light shine before men, is there really any point in blindly obeying an ordinance for the sake of obeying it?

This little book is written not merely to exalt Holy Communion as the highest form of worship for the Christian but to show how, for Christians who are prepared to use their minds and imaginations, it can deepen and enrich their spiritual lives. If, after some years' steady attendance, we find nothing like this happening in our lives, it is wise to call a halt. The fault cannot lie in the rite which Christ instituted, and the vast volume of evidence of all Churches of all ages cannot be airily dismissed. The fault must lie somewhere in ourselves, in our approach, in our way of thinking, or, quite simply, in our lack of preparation. No good will come of growing morbid over this, or calling ourselves bad names; far better calmly and dispassionately to examine our thinking in the light of the facts, to examine our physical, mental and spiritual approach quietly and deliberately. Assuming of course that we are in love and charity with our neighbours, assuming that we are truly sorry for our sins and failures, and assuming that we intend to lead with Christ a new life, the fault must lie either in our lack of comprehension of the meaning of the Sacrament, or in our lack of belief that Christ intends us to meet Him at that point. Half an hour's honest thinking is worth many weary months of coming to Communion out of a sense of duty or respectability and hoping that it will sort itself out. It is to help in this honest thinking that this little book has been written.

ONE

COMMUNION AND COMMONSENSE

'WHAT has poor earth-bound commonsense got to do
with the high mystery of Holy Communion?' One
can readily imagine this question being asked by a
certain type of mind. Of course it cannot be suggested that the awe-inspiring mystery of this Sacra-
men can ever be encompassed by commonsense.
Nevertheless, it is all too easy for certain people to
soar up into the boundless empyrean of religious
fantasy, and too readily to forget the earth upon
which our pilgrimage must be made. To another type
of person, whose feet are solidly set upon the earth,
there appears such a gap between his daily experience
of life and the religious experience of which he has
heard and read that he very easily becomes discour-
aged and gives up the spiritual quest.

Now Holy Communion is concerned with reality
and not at all with religious fantasy. The understanding of even part of its significance will certainly lead
us high above the limitations of commonsense. Yet
though we may be called to transcend our reason, the
religion of Jesus Christ never calls us to contradict
it, and it is no bad thing to make a start from the solid
basis of what we are and what we know to be true.

Let us start by reminding ourselves that Jesus
Christ was a most devastatingly practical Person. On
more than one occasion He brought religious senti-

mentality and fantasy down to earth. His greatest enemies, indeed almost His only enemies, were those who had divorced religion from life and who had retired into a religious world where commonsense values no longer obtained.

The advice that Jesus gave was always sound and practical. Reading the Gospels will show us that so far from urging men to retire from this world and contemplate God, the point that Jesus was continually trying to make was that men should see that the Kingdom of God was in the here and now. He pointed out that our relationship with God was intimately bound up with our relationship with our fellow-men —that we could not expect, for example, the forgiveness of God unless we were prepared to extend forgiveness to those who had wronged us. The commonsense instincts were to be trusted. *'If you then for all your evil know how to give good gifts . . . how much more . . .?'* Life in the here and now was in one sense of eternal significance, for He Himself had linked Himself indissolubly to the life of Man: He said, *'Inasmuch as ye did it not . . . ye did it not unto Me'* (Matthew 25[31-46]).

It was always actual human behaviour that mattered to Jesus and never rosy religious dreams. The young man who hoped to be told what he could add to the pyramid of his spiritual accomplishment was told to sell all he possessed and follow Christ. The man who sought to settle the nice point as to who really was his neighbour was told in effect that whatever human being was in need was his neighbour. The woman who cried out sentimentally, *'How wonderful*

it must be to have been your mother!' was told, *'Yes,
and still more wonderful to hear the Word of God
and keep it'* (Luke 11[27, 28]).

There is always in the life and teaching of Jesus
Christ a note of downright commonsense, of practical
human living. We cannot therefore believe that in
instituting this great Sacrament of His own Body and
Blood, He would for one moment forget the burden
of His teaching. Doubtless, as we shall see, through
this planned contact with Himself there will be times
when the spirit of man rises above earthly things. But
since this life is so constructed that we have always
to return to the humdrum, the unpleasant, the difficult and the ugly, surely this Sacrament was not prim-
arily designed to enable us to take flights of the spirit.
If it means, as it surely must, union with Christ Himself, it cannot avoid meaning sharing something of
His outlook, His life, His work, in the here and now,
so that in the midst of the mystery there will always
be the keynote of commonsense and practicality.

Now it is unfortunately true that emotion can very
readily impair our critical faculties. If our feelings
are skilfully manipulated, as in the film world, by
what is sometimes called a 'tear-jerker', we may find
our normal powers of judgement largely suspended.
If this is true in the world of the film, of the stage, or
of the novel, it is far more true in the religious world,
where the emotions aroused are deeper and more
sacred. That is why a preacher can talk what in fact
is mere fantasy provided he has got his hearers into
the right emotional frame of mind by the proper tone
of voice and the skilful use of religious phrases. That

is why religious films, for example, can be thoroughly badly done, and yet find few critics, at any rate among Christian people, for the very nature of the subject inhibits their powers of criticism. There is much in all our Churches which never meets the criticism it deserves, because of this particular inhibition.

Now the more sacred and intimate the religious subject may be the less we feel able to use our critical faculties. There are in existence some appalling little books about Holy Communion which are quite out of touch both with the life of today and, what is much more important, with the tenor of Christ's own teaching. Yet they are presumably bought and read by the faithful whose critical faculties are temporarily held in abeyance because of the sanctity of the subject.

This book attempts to avoid this writing of religious jargon, this spinning of religious fantasies. The aim is to give thinking men and women, who have their wits about them, good solid reasons for obeying our Lord's intensely practical command to '*Do this in remembrance of Me*'. The working man, the schoolmaster, the business man, the young married couple, the schoolboy or schoolgirl, or any of the others who come to this Holy Sacrament, should know *why* they are coming to meet our Lord in this way. The emotional aspect of the matter has been covered far too many times by far too many little books, and in any case the emotional side of meeting our Lord can probably safely be left to Him. Yet it may prove useful to set out quite simply the sound and solid reasons for regular attendance at this central act of Christian worship.

It should be pointed out, even though it is obvious enough, that this book is not written for scholars, theologians, or even theological students. They are already well catered for, and in any case know where to turn for information. It is written purely and simply for the ordinary people, some of whom are mentioned above, to whom Holy Communion is as much a puzzle as a mystery and, if the truth were told, something of a secret disappointment.

These ordinary Christians feel, and rightly, that here in this Sacrament is something of tremendous importance. They have been taught, and again quite rightly, that to be a regular Communicant is essential to maintain a healthy spiritual life. Some of them, but probably it is only a minority, do find in Holy Communion an intensive act of adoration and self-offering, a sense of sharing in the highest and purest worship of God, the deep and unmistakable strengthening of their own souls, and possibly quite a lot more. But, if the truth were told—and we shall never get anywhere spiritually unless we do tell the truth—there is a good proportion of people to whom Communion is very little more than a sacred duty. Many clergy and ministers know this to be so through the confidences given to them, and they also know that many good and kindly people are only too ready to blame themselves for their failure to appreciate this Sacrament. Indeed, they sometimes make themselves miserable by self-reproach—this holy mystery never seems to mean to them what they have been led to expect, or what they feel it ought to mean. They continue to be Communicants out of a sense of duty or loyalty, but somehow the glowing precious secret which is plainly experienced by others seems to elude them.

Now, few of us can command our own feelings and none of us can command the Spirit which 'bloweth where it listeth'. But we can do something. We can do some good clear thinking, and we can at the very least put ourselves in the position of having satisfying reasons for coming to Communion.

This absolutely essential honesty about the whole matter is often missing even among some of the best Christians. Because of the greatness of this Christ-ordained rite, we find it difficult to admit, even to ourselves, that it could possibly be a disappointment to us. It is fatally easy for nice conscientious people to pretend to believe what in fact they do not believe, and to try to feel what in fact they do not feel. But we cannot make any progress spiritually without the most uncompromising honesty. We could save ourselves and the Church at large a great deal of unhappiness, unreality, and inward dissatisfaction if we dared to use the clean cold sword of truth. If Communion is in fact largely a disappointment to us, let us have the courage to admit to ourselves and to God that this is so. Let us stop saying to ourselves, 'I oughtn't to feel like this'; let us stop belabouring ourselves by saying, 'There must be something wrong with me.' Let us approach this vast and awe-inspiring mystery with honest hearts, inquiring minds, and commonsense.

TWO

THE LIVING THREAD

A GOOD starting-point for any consideration of the Sacrament of Communion is that it is not an idea which has evolved through the centuries, but the keeping of an order, given by Christ Himself, for nearly 2,000 years. With one or two notable exceptions, the Church on the whole has obeyed Christ's command to 'do this in remembrance' of Him.

Now it is plainly not merely a tradition, even though at times it may have been mechanically or perfunctorily observed. It has obviously been, and still is in the growth of the Church, an integral part of its life.

We are not then regarding a mere tradition. Traditions may or may not be valuable. Some of them have indeed held back the progress of a nation for centuries, and we must not lightly forget Christ's damning words when He told the religious leaders of His day that they *made the Word of God of none effect through their tradition*. We in this country have sometimes an undue regard for the traditional. If a tradition is wise, representing the accumulated wisdom of the years and hallowed by generations of usefulness, we are right to pay respect to it. But a tradition may be thoroughly bad, like the former custom of child-marriage in India, or of the binding of small girls' feet in China. There has been a centuries-old tradition for owning slaves or burning witches or even in some countries for getting rid of unwanted infants. We need to be careful in reverencing tradition. We need to be sure that the tradition is in itself a good thing, wisely founded and carried on usefully and meaningfully.

Now, although we have in Holy Communion far more than a tradition, because we have in it something which is alive in itself, yet it has of course a value simply as a tradition, that is, as something men consider worth passing on from generation to generation. But it is unique in that the other end of it is, so to speak, *alive*, intimately joined to the very life of the Son of God Himself. We may perhaps appreciate this better if we compare this living tradition which we possess with some dead relic which we might, but do not in fact, possess. If, for example, we possessed the actual clothes worn by Christ, a lock of His hair, a piece of furniture which He had made while He worker as a carpenter, or even the actual chalice used at the Last Supper, what should we in fact have? A relic of enormous historical value, even a piece of solid visible evidence. We may be sure that there would be those who would go into a kind of reverent trance before such objects. But it is almost certain that, as happens with people being confronted with, shall we say, a pair of shoes worn by Queen Elizabeth, or a pen used by Samuel Pepys, the mind and attention and heart of the beholder would be drawn *towards the past*. Our eyes would inevitably be drawn backwards towards the fact of Christ's earthly existence instead of forwards to His living Presence today.

Pace the Roman Catholic Church, God in His providence has not allowed the survival of actual physical objects. But we have infinitely more than this, for instead of dead relics, however 'authentic' and well-preserved, we have a living life-line, stretching unbroken to Christ Himself. We have all the comfort and security that comes from historic tradition, but instead of being given the sad nostalgia of looking at an object and saying, 'Look, how wonderful, that is what He touched then', we are given an evergreen memorial which says in effect, *'This is what He touches now'*.

At the time of the Reformation in Europe, the Roman Church was full of such gross abuses, particularly those surrounding the Mass, that finally an explosion occurred which detonated other explosions in country after country. In England and other European countries, the reformers worked with fanatical zeal, hacking away, not only abuses, but accretions and ornamentations of all kinds. So anxious were they to return to the primitive meaning of the Lord's Supper, and so anxious were they to avoid the superstitious and magical that they often left of the Holy Communion 'a bare memorial'. Now we may know very well that there is much more than that in this sacred mystery, but it is well worth reflecting what a memorial has been left to us! In the first place it is a first-class piece of Christian evidence, since the most bitter enemy of Christianity would find it impossible to disprove this long tradition of the Church leading right back to its Founder. In the second place, we have, if we use our imaginations for a moment, a kind of holy pipe-line running unbroken through all the Church's vicissitudes back to the Source of Life Himself. And thirdly, even on the bare memorial view, we have behind us a continuous tradition of meeting in fellowship around 'the broken bread and poured-out wine'. Even to the least sensitive and least historically-minded, this is surely a heart-warming and comforting thing.

If we may for a moment still pursue the 'bare memorial' idea, we must see that the most ardent Protestant reformer still left his section of the Church with a good deal. For the memorial is a memorial of the unforgettable Passion of Christ. It is inescapably a memorial of the Body broken and the Blood poured out for the sins of the world—inescapably therefore a wholesome reminder of the cost of man's redemption. And on the most extreme Protestant view we are never deprived of the sense of meeting in most intimate fellowship with the Redeemer Himself and with those whose lives were given to Him.

THREE

MORE THAN MEMORIAL

BUT the Church as a whole has in fact always thought that there was far 'more in it' than a bare memorial. If, for example, we turn to that monumental piece of work which is likely to remain a classic for many years, Gregory Dix's *The Shape of the Liturgy*, we find that quite early in the Church's history its worship centred in the 'Eucharist'. (May I point out in passing that the word 'eucharist' has no particularly ecclesiastical flavour. It means by derivation the act of giving thanks, and became attached to the Christian Church's central act of worship in very early times.) The early Christians found their deepest fellowship with their unseen Lord as well as with one another in what began as a very simple rite. Their thanksgiving, their worship, their prayers, their re-dedications and the strength for the superhuman task which they carried on so courageously were all poured into, or flowed from, this simple, but mysterious Service.

As the centuries passed and the Church became fat, prosperous, and powerful, all sorts of corruptions and abuses crept in. And since the worst corruption is the corruption of the best, it was probably the Holy Communion, or the Eucharist, which had become the most corrupt by the time of the Reformation. Words charged with highest mystical meaning had become words of magic. The very Act of Consecration had become a kind of superior conjuring trick. The Mass had ceased to be fellowship in a deep mystery and had become the complicated performance of a priestly trick. It had become a spectacle to be gaped at instead of a mystery in which all could share, and to some extent understand.

It was against this citadel of priestliness, this horrifying caricature of Christ's intention that the reformers exploded with such violence. (It is worth noting in passing that the very word *hocus-pocus* is a corruption of part of the Consecration words of the Latin Mass, '*hoc est enim corpus meum*'.) Their protest was a revolt against the whole magical bag of tricks with which the Roman Catholic Church had stifled the sublime simplicity of New Testament Christianity. In some Protestant Churches the revolt against anything which seemed to bear the faintest tone of Rome was so violent that some of the reformed Churches were left, as they are today, with little more than the 'bare memorial' which has already been mentioned. Yet there is some evidence of a growing and significant reaction. For although the reformers were perfectly right to get rid of the magical and superstitious element, they forgot in their enthusiasm that there is a superhuman, a mysterious, and a mystical essence behind the simplicity of Christ. It is not difficult to find those nurtured in an ultra-Protestant tradition who feel the barrenness of a mere memorial, and who, though they still feel that Rome is presenting a caricature of the truth, yet would like to see in their own Liturgy more room for colour and mystery, awe and worship. To put it quite bluntly, evangelical Protestants have been so busy saying what the Holy Communion is *not* that they have left themselves sometimes with a sterile bundle of denials, and very little positive doctrine.

At the Reformation the Anglican Church showed a restraint and a wisdom that was surely admirable. For while in the Thirty-Nine Articles the nonsensical magic of transubstantiation is emphatically denied, yet the Holy Communion Service, as set forth in the Book of Common Prayer, is broad enough to allow of a much wider, much deeper, and generally more satisfying interpretation of Holy Communion than a 'bare memorial'.

FOUR

THE ORIGINAL INTENTION

Now the court of appeal of the reformers was Holy Scripture. Although it is obvious from our diverse branches of the Christian Church that honest men can differ very widely in their interpretation of Scripture, yet it is of course perfectly right to go back to the most primitive Source of all, Christ Himself. To plunge straight into the heart of the matter, we have to ask ourselves such questions as these:

What lay in the mind of Christ when He gave the original command?

What was His intention? and again, since He promised to His Church His own Spirit to lead them into all truth:

Where shall we draw the line between the Spirit's intention and the follies and misconceptions of Man?

These are hard questions to answer, but they are the sort of questions we ought to ask and answer honestly for ourselves, taking as wide a view as possible of the trend of the Spirit's working throughout the world-wide Church of Christ. All of us need, from time to time, to shake ourselves free from the particular form of thinking which our branch of the Church has almost imperceptibly formed around us. So far as is humanly possible, we ought to observe and, if conscience and circumstances permit, take part in the usages of other branches of the Church.

Only in this way can we gain some little insight into what is the intention of the Spirit who makes almost all Christians value this Service so highly. Despite the wide divergence of outward ceremony, we can see that it is the same intuitive reverence for this Christ-ordained action which makes one section of the Church regard a daily reception of Christ's Body and Blood essential, while another section regards such receiving as so high and tremendous a privilege that it should only take place occasionally after weeks or even months of preparation of the soul. There is probably more fundamental agreement here than would appear from the wide superficial disparity.

But let us go back for a moment to the actual words of Institution, or to part of them, for this is of course where the bitter controversy has raged most fiercely. According to our Authorized Version, Jesus, after taking the bread, broke it and gave it to the disciples with the words, 'This is my body.' Now the Roman Catholic Church has suffered for centuries from the grave disadvantage of having its Scriptures as well as its Liturgy officially written in Latin. This is a very real disadvantage, for there is a granite-like quality about a Latin sentence which deprives it of any subtlety or nuance. Thus *'Hoc est corpus meum'* means 'This is my body'. It means neither more nor less; it has no overtones nor undertones; it means literally without qualification what it says. Now Jesus, in all probability, spoke in Aramaic, a Semitic language as different from Latin as chalk from cheese, and His words recorded in the Gospels were written in Greek, a language, even in its New Testament form, both fluid and subtle. To have these crucial words frozen into rock-like Latin is almost bound to lead to error. For Jesus, speaking in an oriental language in an oriental setting, we may be quite certain never meant His words to carry the hard, legal, uncompromising flavour which they have to bear in Latin. He said, for example, 'I am the Door', 'I am the true Vine', 'I am the Road' or 'Way', but nobody dreams of taking these words at their face value, or building a vast theological structure upon their absolute literal truth. Yet this is exactly what has happened with '*Hoc est corpus meum*'.

Dr. James Moffatt, in his translation of the New Testament, sensing that the language was figurative, translates, 'This means my body', and any fellow-translator can sympathize with his intention. Jesus did in fact say 'This is my body' but He was not speaking, indeed cannot have been speaking literally, for as He spoke His normal, human, physical body was plainly visible before His disciples' eyes. He was speaking both poetically and prophetically; and only in a mystical sense, as we shall see in a moment, can the words be taken at their face value. We can readily imagine that the Eleven were as puzzled, yes, and even as shocked, as we might be. It is true that it might be not uncommon in those days for a teacher to institute some simple ceremony by which his pupils, meeting for the last time, would be able to remember him in future, yet there is no parallel for such a raw and striking figure as a man offering his own flesh and blood for his own disciples to consume! We remember how in St. John's Gospel Christ claimed to be the Bread of life, and how it disquieted His followers. 'How,' they asked indignantly, 'can this man give us his flesh to eat?' When it came to this sort of crude and intimate simile they were bewildered and offended. It is not unlikely that the disciples found it just as much a cause for astonishment and disquiet at that last tragic meal together.

What appeared to them the supreme disaster of the Crucifixion very shortly afterwards filled their minds, and we simply do not know at what point historically they remembered and obeyed the command to 'Do this in remembrance'. There is, as we all know, a complete blank in the records between the Resurrection appearances and the Ascension of Christ. We simply have no record of what it was that He taught them during that critical period before His physical departure from the earth. We may of course guess that He not only further 'opened to them the Scriptures', but that He also amplified to them the meaning behind the broken bread and the poured-out wine. But this remains a guess, and all we know for certain is that it was not long before they 'continued steadfast in the breaking of bread and prayers'. Now this is where we may reasonably believe that the early Christians found that the words of Christ were actually and mysteriously true. As they met together in His name and broke the bread, they found that it was indeed His body. They found in experience that the vivid and rather shocking picture that He had given them all of eating and drinking His own body and blood came startlingly true for them. In an entirely new sense which they had not previously

27

recognized they found that 'His flesh was meat indeed and His blood was drink indeed'. We cannot therefore be surprised to find that those who have made a close study of the growth of the worship of the Church find it centred in this simple, Christ-instituted, rite.

FIVE

SACRAMENTS IN LIFE

AT this point we may consider a few illustrations from ordinary life to show how intimately yet mysteriously related are the physical and spiritual. We may then see a little more clearly how the simple words of Christ and His familiar action can bear a meaning far beyond purely rational explanation. Here, for instance, are three ordinary things which have very little meaning as physical actions but which may carry with them something far beyond their apparently trivial significance.

(1) Two lovers kiss; to the observer who knows neither of them this may seem a commonplace, meaningless, or indeed rather vulgar gesture. But to the lovers themselves it may convey a meaning far beyond ordinary means of expression.

(2) Two men who have long been at enmity finally shake hands in reconciliation. Again, to the observer the mere physical action is not worth noticing, but it may be full of the profoundest significance, reaching out in time far beyond the few seconds of the handclasp.

(3) We may take the clapping of hands as a token of love, admiration, or appreciation of some great deed or difficult accomplishment. To a stranger to this planet the beating of hands together would appear ridiculous and would convey absolutely nothing

of the emotional state which this rather odd action is expressing.

Then we may consider not actions, but *things* which become highly charged with emotion, though scientifically speaking they remain exactly the same. Here are three examples:

First a wedding-cake, which is in outward appearance and by every scientific measurement exactly the same cake as it was when it stood in the confectioner's window. But it is now a wedding-cake, used and consumed at the wedding of two people much in love with one another. In one sense, the scientific sense, the cake is not changed, but in the sense of experience it is now Bill's and Joan's wedding-cake, and to the friends, near or far, who eat it, it is quite a different thing from the same cake in a shop window.

Or, let us look at this old armchair. To the eyes of the second-hand furniture dealer it is worth perhaps only a few shillings, but to the sons and daughters of the family it is 'mother's armchair'. It is not merely special, but actually sacred to them because of its hallowed associations.

Or, we may take a Victoria Cross, worth as metal not more than a few pence, but to the parents of the man who died winning it worth something beyond price.

Here, we see, are ordinary inanimate things invested with a particular significance and sanctity because of their association with the love and sacrifice of human beings.

Moreover, there are in this bewildering world in which we find ourselves set, things which strike deep spiritual chords within us, which are not explainable in scientific or rational terms. Music can be analysed into all its resonances, fundamental and harmonic, and its rhythm and pattern explained, but there has never been any explanation of the ways in which it can stir and haunt a human soul. The surge and thunder of the sea, the smell of wood-smoke, the woods carpeted with bluebells, and a hundred other things can touch and move our spirits in a way Science is powerless to explain. It is as though there is another dimension, perhaps several other dimensions, to which our human spirits in some degree respond.

From such things we see that the commonplace may be invested with the highest and purest emotion, and that there are depths and heights in our spirits which may be touched by the simplest of natural phenomena. Then we may well begin to suspect that this physical world is in fact shot through and through with spiritual realities. The physical is plainly often necessary in order to experience or express the spiritual, and what we call the physical may only be the outcrop in time and space of what are eternal realities.

Then we may begin to see the necessity of the Word becoming flesh. For since we cannot appreciate goodness, truth, or beauty until they are embodied in a thing or a person or an action, neither can we properly know the supreme Reality, God, until He becomes a Man and lives among us.

Suppose then, that Jesus, not guessing and fumbling as we so often are, but knowing fully about the inter-relation of the physical and the spiritual, took the ordinary universal things of life on earth and made them do duty for heavenly realities. Then we begin to see how woefully far behind and wide of the mark is the crude magic of transubstantiation. For God does not present us with an unending series of conjuring tricks, but deliberately chooses a fraction of earthly life and uses it as a planned focal point of the real spiritual life. If this is true, and the more you think about it the more likely it seems to be true, then we can hardly be surprised that the early Church found in their simple Eucharist the centre of both their worship of and their contact with the unseen Master.

SIX

TRADITIONAL PREJUDICE

IT is worth noting that we in the Protestant Churches have inherited an anti-Roman tradition stronger than we sometimes realize. This is quite understandable, for Rome has not changed through the centuries and many of the same causes which precipitated the Reformation exist in the Roman Church today. Yet since, as has already been said, the very storm-centre of the disagreement with Rome lies in what Christ meant by the words, 'This is My Body, this is My Blood', we Protestants, if we are not careful, find ourselves loth to believe the real truth of Christ's words and His real Presence in the Sacrament. For example, it is quite common to find people of the strongest Protestant views investing a lock of hair, a book, or even a place with a sacred and even mystical significance. They may stand, for example, with bowed head and most reverent thoughts before the Bible that So-and-so the famous preacher used. They may visit, almost as if on a pilgrimage, the place where such-and-such a sermon was delivered, or such-and-such a book was written. Yet so strong is the anti-Roman feeling in the Protestant Churches that there is still a very great reluctance to accord to the sacred elements in Holy Communion their proper mystical significance. This surely is a profound mistake. If we, for all our blindness, have enough sense and intuition to know that the spiritual can and does inter-penetrate the material and thereby change the significance of perfectly ordinary things, with how much more reverence ought we to regard the bread and wine consecrated in Christ's Name to be His Body and Blood for us who believe in Him?

It would seem that Christ, knowing that we have this sense and intuition, chose with sublime simplicity a fellowship rite, the meaning of which would, for all its apparent simplicity, meet the needs of His followers 'till He come'. It would be a thousand pities if we allowed a controversy which is now more than four hundred years old to close our minds against *His* intention. We may note here in passing that this Christ-ordained Ceremony is meant for the nourishment and inspiration of the earthly army of His followers only 'till He come'. When the Complete swallows up the Incomplete, when faith is replaced by sight, when the battle is over, there will be neither point nor need for the continuing of this Holy Meal. This needs to be said because one sometimes comes across a conception of Heaven which resembles nothing so much as a Choral Eucharist raised to the nth degree! But of course this cannot be a true one. In the actual presence of the King the need for the symbols, even the holiest and most mythical, disappears instantly. The Eucharist is a profound and marvellous mystery so long as we walk by faith and not by sight, but it is a ceremony belonging to this world only; we show forth the Lord's death only 'till He come'.

Heaven is of course represented in the New Testament more than once as a 'feast' or as a 'marriage feast'. But this is quite a different picture from that of a sacrificial meal. The Heavenly Feast represents the rejoicing, the reunion, and the triumph, when the whole present scheme of redemption is complete.

Let us look again at the words of Christ. Of the bread He said, 'This is My Body', and of the wine He said, 'This is My Blood', and it was so. Long before superstitions and abuses crept in, the early Christians found these words came true, and very naturally built their fellowship and communion around this mystery. Let us try to look at it, if we can, with fresh, unbiased eyes. This is the planned meeting-place of time and space with Real Life—the Life of God. This is the designed focal point where spiritual and material meet.

It is often useful to use unfamiliar phrases and points of view in order to grasp the truth afresh. Let us forget then for a moment the doctrines, the technical terms, the jargon, even the customs and traditions of our particular branch of the Christian Church. Can we not see that here is a guaranteed contact with underlying Reality? Or, to change the picture, here is a tiny chink in our mortal life through which streams the pure Light of Heaven. Or, if you will not think this an extravagant picture, here is a flower of heavenly species blooming in our mortal soil for you and me to pick and take away. These and other not so familiar pictures may help us to grasp the other-worldly quality of what is offered to us in this world's aspect. But the sheer truth of the matter is much more soul-shattering than any figure of

speech for—let it break over us afresh—here is the
Son of God Himself saying, 'Take, eat, this is My
Body: drink this, it is My Blood.'

Pictures and figures, especially unhackneyed ones,
may lead us onward and upward in expectancy, but
we are scarcely prepared for the Reality when it
bursts upon us, for God is no longer far away, no
longer the unseen and rather vague Companion; the
Eternal is in the here and now, flinging aside His
majesty and narrowing Himself to fit our need!

'Walking by faith', the life to which we are called,
is sometimes lonely and dark; there are many puzzles
and many uncertainties, but here at this point there
is no uncertainty and no puzzlement. Here there is a
hole in the blanket of our dark. With incredible quiet
and almost intolerable humility God Himself is always here to meet us.

Let us look for a moment at the symbols themselves. They are reminiscent of, and consistent with,
that strange, disturbing humbleness of the Incarnation. That quiet, lonely entry into the stream of
human history is not what we should have planned
or imagined for the entry of the Son of God, and
neither are these commonplace symbols what we
should have planned or expected for the entry of
Glory into our workaday world. It is the King's feast;
but we are offered, not frosted cake, but unleavened
bread, and broken at that. We are offered no vintage
wine, but the ordinary wine of the days of His
humanity, poured out in simplicity. This humility is
all of a piece with the manger, the carpenter's shop,
the ride on the donkey, and the Cross of wood. The

majesty and magnificence lie, not in the symbols, but in the generosity of the Giver.

Even more piercing still than this pride-destroying humility is the fact that God is offering us, not a jewel from His treasures, but Himself in His vulnerable, refusable, crucifiable Love.

We may well start back at this breath-taking generosity. We are prepared to think of God as Power, and Glory, and Justice, and Holiness, but somehow our hearts and minds are shy of Him as naked, vulnerable Love; yet that is how He offers Himself to us.

SEVEN

THE NATURE OF
THE FELLOWSHIP

THE fellowship to which we are called in this strange and honouring and humbling gift of God is inescapably a fellowship of Love which may easily mean a fellowship of suffering. There is joy and strength, of course, in this holy food and drink, but it is also an inevitable joining forces with the vast Scheme of reconciliation and redemption. Now there is something in our natural selves that may well make us wary of such a contact. The man who in his heart intends to go on being selfish or proud, or who has already decided how far his Christian convictions should carry him, is probably obeying a sound instinct when he keeps away from this glorious but perilous Sacrament. For, if the truth be told, men are often willing to put their trust in a god who in the end must be triumphant, simply because they want to be on the winning side; but they are not nearly so ready to bear any part of the cost of that winning. Yet the fellowship of the broken bread and the poured-out wine can mean no less than that.

Christians of every kind need to beware of pietistic individualism, and this is no less true at this focal point of worship than at any other place in the Christian life. That is why what is called High Mass,

which is pre-eminently a spectacle, must always fall
short of Christ's intention. For Holy Communion
was from the beginning a fellowship meal, not merely
a fellowship between each individual soul with its
God, but a fellowship in love and willingness to bear
pain between those who love Christ. There have been
some experiments in the Anglican Church made with
the intention of strengthening this sense of fellowship. The Altar has sometimes been moved and the
Celebrant stands at the east side facing the people.
Sometimes it has been arranged that the fellowship
of believers kneel on three sides at least of the Altar,
so that it becomes far more the Lord's Table than
when it is merely gazed at as a focal point of reverence against the east end of a Church, however useful
that may be. But whatever is done outwardly, it is
important that Christians should recover and re-
emphasize in their own thoughts and prayers the
basic idea of fellowship.

All meals have a fellowship value: we know
people better when they have come to tea with us, for
example. The man of the world who says to his
friends, 'Come and have a drink with me', is obeying
a deep human instinct for the sacramental, however
crudely we may think he expresses it. But this particular fellowship is naturally of a deeper and more
important kind. We must not for a moment belittle
the value of ordinary human social intercourse,
whether it be held in connexion with the Church or
not. But here Christ Himself is inviting us to experience and enjoy normal human fellowship at a
much deeper level. Together we are satisfying a com-

mon spiritual need; together we are re-dedicating our lives to the service of Christ with all that that may imply. Together we are making use of this Christ-appointed contact and opportunity. The fellowship may not express itself in a hearty back-slapping way, but it should surely be expressed in a renewed sense of family solidarity. We are meeting together at one of the deepest levels open to us as human beings.

Holy Communion is surely always falling short of its true purpose if it fails to produce some sense of solidarity with our fellow-worshippers. It must never be regarded as a luxury for the devout; high and mysterious though it is, it is also the ordained place of deepest fellowship for those who are committed to the Way of Christ, ordinary, faulty, and imperfect though they are.

EIGHT

SPIRITUAL NUTRITION

THE more we look at, and in experience share in, this bright mystery the more we are conscious that it has many facets. It may be possible for some rare souls to hold in their minds simultaneously many aspects of the Holy Mystery, but for most of us it will seem that one facet or another is caught by the light, according to our need or according to our spiritual growth. In this small book we are trying to look at a few of the many aspects by which this Sacrament reaches human hearts and satisfies human needs. Let us now turn to a particular aspect, that of God giving Himself to us in a special and, as it were, concentrated way. It is perfectly true that the Love of God exerts a gentle but continuous pressure upon human life all the time, and breaks through wherever the insulation of the purely materialistic wears thin.

But although all life is lived in the sight of God, we cannot consciously remember this all the time, and therefore we set aside a time in our busy lives when we remind ourselves of great realities and open our lives afresh to the Spirit of God. Every day should be a day of worship, prayer, and praise, but because human nature is so often dulled and blanketed by the world's stifling pressures, Christians choose one day of the week to keep especially for God. All that we possess belongs to God in the last resort, but many Christians find it a salutary reminder to set aside a tenth or some other proportion of their income so that thereby the whole may be hallowed. Following the same principle, we may observe that the Christian Church as a whole, while not forgetting that every part of life is really sacramental, regards this Christ-instituted action as an especially focused and concentrated way of receiving God. Here in a particularly memorable and intimate way God meets and feeds us by His appointment where spiritual and physical concur.

Now we have already noticed something of the strong mystical significance of the symbols, but they are of course not merely to be thought about or looked at—they are meant to be absorbed into ourselves. It was surely a sound instinct which made the reformers reject the Roman debasement of Holy Communion into the spectacle of the Mass. In the Anglican Church, Article 25 still speaks good sense:

> *The Sacraments were not ordained of Christ to be gazed upon or to be carried about,* **but** *that we should duly use them and in such only as worthily receive the same they have a wholesome effect or operation.*

We are all familiar with the mystery of ordinary physical digestion. Indeed, like a good many commonplace happenings of this life, we are so familiar with it that we fail to see its wonder. A, B, and C sit round a breakfast table and from the same packet of corn-flakes, the same bowl of sugar, and the same jug of milk they all break their fast. By a very complex process and, in the last resort, by a mystery which no one can explain, the inanimate matter eaten by A becomes part of A, rebuilding his tissues, or providing him with energy, or slowly adding to his weight. Exactly the same inanimate physical materials become by a similar process part of B or C. Now A may be red-haired, B may be blond, C may be completely bald, yet the taking of precisely similar quantities of food makes no alteration to their characteristics, but simply becomes part of the physical bodies of A, B, and C. This sort of thing has happened so many million times that we have forgotten that it is not only a highly complex process but a very mysterious one. Now here in this holy Sacrament we are asked to believe a greater wonder—greater not so much in degree as in quality. We are in fact asked to believe that through the commonplace miracle of physical absorption and nutrition God Himself quickens and nourishes the spiritual life within us. We cannot help thinking at once of the words of Christ in St. John's Gospel, 'Except ye eat my flesh and drink my blood ye have no life in you' (John 6[53]). The absorption of Christ into the human soul is an utter necessity if a human being is to remain a Christian at all.

These words spoken by Christ have an obviously wider application than to the Sacrament of Holy Communion. A man may absorb Christ through meditation and contemplation, through the opening of his spirit to the Holy Spirit, by his communion and prayer and worship in his own private room with the living Christ. And yet it is difficult to avoid the conclusion that though Christ was speaking in the broadest possible way of feeding on Himself, He did have in mind the concentrated absorption of Himself which He appointed in the Memorial Meal.

Now the burden of the Pauline Epistles is of a supernatural quality of life which men and women of quite ordinary calibre can live by reason of Christ Himself living in them. It is a truth we need to recapture on a grand scale in these days. We diminish the splendour and power of the Gospel when we reduce the Christian Faith to a rule of life or a strenuous effort of following the Way. We do not reckon nearly enough on the power available through the Christ who lives in us. We may think it is reverence for the Person of our Lord which makes us shy about conceiving Him as living and operative in our imperfect personalities. But this is a false reverence, like that false reverence that will not really accept the perfectly genuine humanity of Jesus Christ. We really show irreverence, we really dishonour Christ, when we refuse to believe that His Life, with its transforming and activating powers, can be resident in such people as ourselves. This is, declares St. Paul, a secret which has been hidden from so many generations, but is now perfectly clear (Colossians 1[26]). God is no longer to be thought of as the external God, to be pleased, or placated, or feared, or slavishly obeyed. The new Plan, the new scheme of things is 'Christ in you, the hope of glory'.

NINE

THE CHRIST WITHIN US

IF we can accept the statement that Christ lives within us, not as a kind of helpful metaphor, but as a sober literal fact (for that is what the New Testament teaches), it is only a step to realize that this supernatural element within us needs to be maintained by every possible means. Certainly the most important thing is to believe that it is true, that God does so honour us by placing something of His own Personality within our imperfect selves. But the cares and anxieties of this world will not only tend to make this seem a fantastic belief, but will also, if we allow them, starve out this supernatural life almost to the point of extinction.

The recollection of God, the worship of God with mind as well as heart, sincere prayer, and thanksgiving will all help to maintain the vigour of the Christ-life within us. But for inner nourishment can there be anything more appropriate than the bread and wine which Christ Himself declared to be His own Body and Blood?

Now it is obvious that the Christian life can be maintained without Holy Communion at all. Indeed it is so maintained, for example, by both the Quakers and the Salvation Army. But it is surely not the normal, surely not the 'Catholic' way (in its proper sense), in which the Spirit has led the Church through the centuries. A man may lead a happy and useful life with only one lung, or with part of his internal organs removed by surgery, but that is not the norm. Obviously it is possible for God to give His grace in a dozen different ways, but it is difficult to see why Christ instituted this particular means of spiritual nutrition, unless it had a particular point and purpose for the vast army of His future followers. Indeed it is true to say from experience that Christians, unless they are prejudiced, or conditioned by their upbringing, are drawn intuitively towards Holy Communion. Their own natural spiritual hunger draws them instinctively towards the holy provision of the Lord's Table.

All Christians know with sorrow the difference between their high vocation and their everyday failures. All Christians recognize the need for the continual reinforcement of the good and timeless element within their personalities. Here in the Sacrament, under cover of what is ordinary, Christ is prepared to do the extraordinary—to infuse fresh life, to heal, to stimulate, to provide that health of soul which is one of the important meanings of 'holiness'.

All healing of the body is really accomplished by the *vis medicatrix naturae*, the healing force of nature. The most that medicine and surgery can do is to give this natural force a chance to overcome disease. As we all know very well, in the healthy body there is a host of minor ills which is overcome by the natural force of healing without recourse to doctor or medicine. Similarly the healthy and vigorous mind rejects the unwholesome and copes valiantly with the difficult. It is surely not unreasonable to suppose that there is a *vis medicatrix naturae* of the soul which is quite capable of dealing with the temptations, the sins, and the setbacks of the spiritual life. But only a healthy, properly-nourished soul can exert this force, and the Christ-life within us needs its own particular nourishment to retain its resilience and vigour. It surely follows then that to receive with faith this Holy Food is adding immeasurably to the health and strength of the innermost soul.

As we imagine ourselves reverently kneeling to receive the sacred elements, among the helpful pictures which we may hold in our minds are these:

(a) Here am I, mortal and faulty, yet called through Christ to be and live as a son of God. I am called to a life of supernatural character. Of myself I readily run short of love, patience, peace of mind, and many other spiritual qualities. I know that by myself I have not sufficient spiritual resilience or spiritual initiative to live as a son of God. Yet I also know, since the New Testament is so emphatic on the subject, that within me there lives the very Life of Christ. Therefore, deliberately, willingly, and expectantly I open the inner shrine of my personality to receive more of this fresh life. I go through the physical motions of eating and drinking, which I have known since I was a child, and I believe that in this familiar and universal action God re-invigorates the Christ-life within me.

(*b*) I accept these sacred elements with the deepest reverence of which I am capable. For just as no early disciple could forget the shadow of impending death under which this rite was established, so I cannot forget that herein lies the costly Pledge of my reconciliation with God. If I accept it, and receive it into my inmost being, I am accepting that great gift of reconciliation, that restoration of relationship between the Infinite God and my soiled self which by myself I am powerless to make. It is true that Christians all over the world are receiving a similar Pledge, which means, as we have seen, a deep sense of fellowship, but there is a sense in which God here meets the individual in his individuality. Paul knew well how long and deep and wide and high was the Love of God, yet there were times when he felt that same redeeming love sharpened to the point of individual contact. 'The Son of God, who loved me and gave Himself for me', he wrote. In the same way I may feel and accept the gift of reconciliation in Christ, focused for me personally as I receive my share of the holy Bread and Wine.

(*c*) As every pilgrim in the spiritual life knows, it is hard to hold the unseen in our mental and spiritual grasp. Visions of eternal truth, crystal clear at the time, have a disconcerting way of fading from our memory. But here I may re-assure myself. Here I know that Christ Himself, taking pity on our blindness, and understanding our limitations, is allowing the seen and the unseen, the material and the spiritual, to coincide. Here, by His appointment, I can receive and absorb things that are physical and know that they are really things which are spiritual. It is no mere piece of bread or sip of wine that I receive—I receive the very Body and Blood of Christ into my own imperfect self.

TEN

CHRIST AND THE REAL SELF

WE have just been considering spiritual nutrition, the maintenance of a vigorous Christ-life within ourselves. We must do a little thinking here or we may fog the mind with a confused picture, and a clear mental picture, however simple, will usually help us when we are dealing with spiritual things.

For example, it might be questioned in the foregoing chapter whether we are to think of the Holy Food as nourishing the life of Christ within us or whether it is our own souls which are feeding on the 'Bread of the world in mercy broken'. Here, let us put forward the bold suggestion that our 'real selves', our 'souls', and the 'Christ within us' are essentially the same thing. We shall certainly find support for this view in the teaching of the New Testament. First, let us establish the fact that there is a 'real self' within us all. If there were not, there would be nothing in Matthew, Peter, James, and John, and the millions since their day, to respond to the One who says, 'Follow Me.' There is no need to stress here the reality of the other factors within us; we are only too well aware of them. But it would appear from the record of the Gospels that Christ invariably addressed Himself to the real person existing behind the façade presented to the world. Even His scathing onslaughts against the hypocrisy of the religious leaders may fairly be regarded as an 'armour-piercing' method designed to reach the diminished but real person within.

Now when the real person, either suddenly or gradually, decides to follow Christ, he experiences not only a sense of peace, forgiveness, and deep happiness, but also of being, in a previously unimagined way, in touch with the Infinite God. Small, poor, and flickering his flame may be, but in all humility he recognizes that it is a tiny part of the celestial Radiance.

Christ Himself plainly taught that His own life and those of His close disciples were interwoven not only with each other but even with the eternal life of the Father. Familiarity has dulled for most of us that hitherto unheard-of intimacy between the life of God, the life of Christ, and the life of the disciples of Christ, which is spoken of as a plain matter of fact in, for example, chapters 14, 15, and 16 of St. John's Gospel. Like many other of the New Testament promises, we tend to think of these things as too good to be true, and cannot see that they are both good and true. The life of the Vine, for example, and the life of the branches is of the same stuff, essence, and quality. It cannot therefore be impertinent for us to hold firmly to the belief that the life of our real selves is the same thing as the life of Christ within us.

The letters of the New Testament abound not with pious hopes but with audacious certainty. 'Now are we the sons of God', 'heirs of God and joint-heirs with Christ', seated together with Christ—these are the sort of expressions which sparkle on the sea of that early Christian confidence. God is now no longer aloof, separate—He is one with His sons. Confidence that man could never muster, certainty which he never dared to believe possible—all this and much more has come true in Christ, and shines from the pages of these unselfconscious writings.

But we, in our cautious reverence, forget how closely God in Christ has identified Himself with humanity. Because of our worldly set of values, we set God on the wrong kind of pedestal, so that the reality of the Incarnation becomes as impossible to conceive as the thought of a high-ranking Civil Servant having tea with his office-cleaner! If we do that sort of thing, and ascribe this world's dignity and privilege to God (which is a frightful piece of impertinence), we miss the whole point of God's pride-shattering humility. But there is no blinking the facts. God *did* become Man, God *did* accept the limitation and frustrations of human living, God *did* link Himself indissolubly with poor blundering humanity. He did not shrink from calling Himself, and acting as though He were, Representative Man, which is what 'Son of Man' means. Moreover, in that picture of the Last Judgement, commonly known as the parable of the Sheep and the Goats, He so far identifies Himself with needy suffering human beings as to state categorically that the way in which men treat each other is in solemn fact the way in which they treat Him (Matthew 25[40–6]).

In the light then of God's deliberate identification of Himself with mortal man through Christ, we shall not go far wrong if we identify the Christ who is formed and is developing within us with the real self which has heard and is responding to His call. We need this particular nourishment, for upon the health of this vital centre depends the whole quality of our life.

ELEVEN

RE-PRESENTATION OR REPRESENTATION

No one could possibly attend Holy Communion in any Church without sensing its profound and mysterious undertones of sacrifice. But we are bound to stop and ask ourselves such questions as these:

'Is the sacred rite itself a literal sacrifice? Is the priest or minister re-presenting to God, on behalf of himself and his people, the one perfect Sacrifice?'

It is of course on this point that 'Catholics' and 'Protestants' fundamentally disagree. The Catholic, sensing the awe-full holiness of God and the utter unworthiness of man to approach Him, feels strongly that in this Christ-appointed Service he has far more than a memorial. Since the Bread and Wine after consecration are the very Body and Blood, he is in solemn truth pleading before God for his acceptance. The priest is offering the only Sacrifice, by re-presenting the sacred Body and Blood of the Son of God Himself. To the Protestant this line of thinking often appears little short of blasphemous. He too is conscious of the awe-full holiness of God, and of his own sinfulness. He too knows that the only way of reconciliation with God is through the sacrifice of Christ. Yet he believes most fervently that 'Christ *once* hath suffered, the just for the unjust, to bring us to God'. The Anglican reformers left no loophole for misunderstanding on this point. The reconciliatory act on the Cross can never be repeated, and the Anglican Consecration Prayer states with unmistakable emphasis that Christ 'made there (by His one oblation of Himself once offered) a full, perfect, and sufficient sacrifice, oblation, and satisfaction, for the sins of the whole world'.

If the Catholic attempt to re-present the Sacrifice appears blasphemous, it is of course intentionally nothing of the kind. Even the strongest Protestant would agree that Christ's supreme Act of Reconciliation is a demonstration in human history of what is eternally true in the attitude of God towards mankind. It is impossible to believe that the best kind of Catholic is really trying to add to what can never be added to. It could be said that in most cases he has been indoctrinated with the idea that God can only be approached by man through the Sacrifice of Christ (a truth on which all Christians agree): but also— and this is where to the Protestant mind he is sadly misled—he appears to have been taught that God requires a continual stream of sacrifices in order to maintain His attitude of benevolence towards sinful men. The Catholic surely errs, not in his sense of God's holiness nor in his sense of man's unworthiness and sinfulness, but in the implied thought that God requires periodical reminders, and worse than that, continual re-presentations, of the One Perfect Sacrifice. If the Catholic could for a little while stand aside from his habitual mode of thought, and free himself from years of indoctrination on this particular point, he might see what a caricature of the Love of God these endless re-presentations of the one great Sacrifice imply. At best they seem to the Protestant mind to suggest that the tremendous magnificent God whom Christians worship must be reminded of the sacrifice of His own Son (as though He could possibly forget!), and at the worst they imply a kind of talismanic placation of an otherwise angry God, which is far more heathen than Christian.

The truth is surely that it is *we* who need to be reminded of the cost of our redemption, but never God. There are prayers in many liturgies which ask God to 'remember' this or that. This may be admitted as a figure of speech, such as indeed the language of prayer must contain, but when it becomes a solemn and solid doctrine it becomes perilous. Have we so little confidence in the Love of God and of His own almost incredible reconciliatory action in Christ that we must use these sacred mysteries to remind Him and secure our own acceptance in the Beloved? It is as monstrous as to think of an earthly son who could never approach his father unless there was a due recital of all the undeserved benefits which the son had received from his father; or as though a man who had been saved from drowning many years ago by his friend could never enjoy fellowship with that friend unless the story of the rescue were first gratefully recounted.

Those whose minds tend towards the 'Catholic' way of thinking may think the above words severe or even unjust, but surely they are a perfectly fair description of the impression that Catholic faith and worship gives to the open-minded Protestant. The Protestant would indeed be glad to hear that he is mistaken, and that the Catholic does in fact confidently accept access to God through Christ, the one Mediator, without recourse to Mass or Priest. But meanwhile he holds that the Reformation was an absolute necessity for the preservation of New Testament Christianity. His attitude towards the sacrifice of Christ upon the Cross is best expressed in the words of the author of the Epistle to the Hebrews:

Christ is not entered into the holy places made with hands, which are the figures of the true, but into heaven itself, now to appear in the presence of God for us; nor yet that he should offer himself often, as the high priest entereth into the holy place every year with blood of others; for then must he often have suffered since the foundation of the world; but now once in the end of the world hath he appeared to put away sin by the sacrifice of himself (Hebrews 9[24-6]).

TWELVE

THE UNIQUE SACRIFICE

ALL sincere Christians are deeply grieved by what the Anglican Book of Common Prayer calls 'our unhappy divisions'. Most unhappily and regrettably the deepest cleavage between the two main bodies of Christian thought, i.e. 'Protestant' and 'Catholic', occurs in the doctrine surrounding the most holy and intimate mystery of the Body and Blood of Christ. It is a truly shocking thought that at this point, which in early days was the natural centre of worship and fellowship, there has been the most bitter controversy and cruel persecution. That this is so must grieve both Protestant and Catholic Christians alike.

It always appears to the Protestant mind that the Catholic emphasis on the sacrificial aspect of the Mass means that the Priest is attempting not to *represent*, but actually to *re-present* the unique Sacrifice of Christ. He appears to be taking upon himself to plead a sacrifice before God, who surely has Himself already made, in the Person of His Son, the only sacrifice that could ever reconcile Man and God. Now all Christians would surely agree that *we* need to be reminded of the cost of our redemption, *we* need to be reminded that Christ is humble enough to give Himself to us in these meaningful symbols, *we* need to be reminded that we are called cheerfully to share the life of the One whose Body was broken and whose Blood was shed for the world's redemption. But God cannot possibly need to be reminded, and the exuberant vitality of the New Testament Letters shows no hint of such pleading or such reminder. Indeed, there is an exhilarated confidence because men now have unrestricted access to God through Christ. They now have peace with God. 'There is no condemnation for those who are in Christ Jesus.' There is every indication that such joy and abounding confidence is only possible through Christ, but there is not the faintest hint that the Sacrifice once accepted by mind and heart needs to be repeated: there is no suggestion that Almighty God can only be safely approached through a ritual act. In all sincerity the Protestant cannot help noticing the sharp difference between the joyous assurance of the New Testament letters and the implication, whether intentional or not, that God can only safely be approached through the Mass.

To build up in the mind the idea of a God who is only periodically reconciled to us through repeated 'sacrifices', suggests not only a false picture of God our Father, but a fatal split in the Personality of the Almighty Himself. Paul was surely inspired when he wrote, 'God was in Christ reconciling the world unto Himself', for the initiative of redemption and reconciliation has only one source, the Love of God. It was necessary in the economy of sinful human history for God to become a man, for Him to offer a life of perfect obedience, for Him to effect reconciliation by allowing Himself to be caught up in the sin-and-death process; it was necessary for Him to 'taste death for every man' as well as to shatter resoundingly the strength of sin and death. But that must not for one moment lead us to suppose that there is a dichotomy in the Divine Nature. It is God who sends His Son, it is God who reconciles the world unto Himself, it is God 'in whom we have redemption through His (Christ's) blood'. Moreover, it is God who through His Spirit makes the reconciliation not only theoretically possible, but practicably and even consciously acceptable in the mind and heart of the Christian.

We cannot help reflecting that the Catholic doctrine of 'pleading the sacrifice of Christ' is all part of that unhappy refusal really to accept the Good News, that we are the sons of God. It is heathen gods who need continual propitiation, and it is a relic from paganism which will not accept as a *fait accompli* the strange work of Christ.

Now it is perfectly true that we cannot earn our salvation. No work of ours and no repentances of ours can do more than erect a rather shaky bridge-head towards the beauty and holiness of God. But the glory of the Good News is that the bridge has been built, peace has been made. Nothing can now separate us from the Love of God. If the mystery of Holy Communion reminds us of the Love of God and, in a kind of acted parable, if it reminds us of the cost of our redemption, well and good. It can be, indeed it should be, a representation of a tremendous act on the part of Almighty God. But it can never be a re-presentation, or we at once lose our solid standing in Christ, and we belittle, however unconsciously, the splendid generosity of God. Holy Com-

munion then is not literally a sacrifice at all; it is a
visible acted parable and it is analogous to uplifting
Christ, proclaiming the Cross, an unforgettable show-
ing of the Character of the God whom we adore. St.
Paul wrote (1 Corinthians 11[26]), 'For as oft as ye eat
this bread and drink this cup, ye do show forth the
Lord's death till He come.' The word translated
'show' is equivalent to 'announce', 'proclaim', even
'advertise'. The celebrating of the Holy Communion
is a proclaiming of the Gospel, not merely a potent
reminder but the deliberate proclaiming of an infinitely costly Act. Because of this, it is by no means
unknown, where this mysterious rite is reverently
carried through, for people to be not merely spiritually quickened, but to be aware for the first time of
the real relationship between Man and God, and to
be converted in the truest sense of that word.

In this Sacrament, then, we approach God by
virtue of His own Self-giving. There is a deceptive
gentleness and simplicity about this, as in so many
of the ways of God. But just as love so often begets
love, so sacrifice begets sacrifice, and in the presence
of this simple but profound reminder of Christ's perfect Sacrifice men and women are often moved to
offer themselves afresh to God, whatever the personal
cost may mean. In this sense only, every celebration
of the Communion is a sacrifice—the proclaimed
and uplifted Sacrifice, so simply but powerfully represented, meeting with the response of human lives
prepared to serve God sacrificially.

There is then an inescapable note of sacrifice per-
meating this mystery. There are other aspects of this

Holy Communion, as has been suggested elsewhere in this little book, but this is central and essential. As far as God is concerned there is naturally not the slightest variation of His attitude towards us; it is always that of patient unremitting love. But we, though we can and should enjoy the utmost confidence in God through reconciliation of Christ, need not so much to be reminded of our status, as to be re-orientated in our attitude of mind. To be frank, we can easily lapse into carelessness, and even casualness, toward the Love of God. We can easily forget, even if we do not intentionally evade, the sacrificial nature of our calling. Therefore regularly and reverently 'we show the Lord's death', both as a salutary reminder of our redemption and as a provocation of our own willing and loving service.

The word 'altar' (which because of its Roman associations does not appear in the Anglican Book of Common Prayer) may surely be used as at least a striking figure of speech. In common use it means the place of offering, and that not only in the propitiatory sense. When Christ told us to leave our gift at the 'altar' and to be reconciled to our brother before we made our gift, I do not suppose for one moment that He was thinking of the gift as propitiary; the altar is simply the place where a gift, a sacrificial gift, is offered. Not literally, then, as we have seen, but figuratively, the Lord's Table is the place where the Lord's own Body and Blood are shown as His all-embracing Sacrifice for mankind. By the same figure, we in return lay ourselves, our souls and bodies, indeed all that we have and are, upon His Altar to be used in His service. And it is perhaps worth remarking that just as we recognize that a sacrificial gift once made cannot be withdrawn, so, as we reciprocate in our poor measure that tremendous Love, we commit ourselves without thought of retraction or reservation. But because the best of us are weak and sinful, and are easily seduced by our own self-will or the values of the world around us, we need to renew that act of sacrifice, perhaps more often than we think, upon the altar of God's service.

THIRTEEN

PREPARATION—
BODY AND MIND

'THE world is too much with us', wrote Wordsworth over a century ago, and surely the tensions of contemporary anxiety and the pressures of contemporary thinking are nearer to today's Christian than ever before. If he is to maintain the spiritual life within him, he must by desperate resolution elbow out a space in his daily activities when he can obey the command to 'Be still and know that I am God'. If he fails to do this, if he fails to make room for prayer and worship, for the thoughtful reading of the New Testament and for the intelligent receiving of the Body and Blood of Christ, he will be moulded little by little into the world's pattern—which is the precise opposite of what is supposed to happen to a Christian.

Now from the busy, hustling, worldly point of view, the life of the spirit will always appear to be a waste of time. On the other hand, in those rare moments when we have succeeded in achieving something like a spiritual point of view, we wonder why we sweat and strive and give so much of our precious selves to the passing things of time. Most of us, if we are Christian at all at heart, know that it is the maintenance of this inner life which is of the greatest importance. Jesus with clear insight put His finger right on the spot when he said, 'What shall it profit a man if he shall gain the whole world and lose his own soul?' (Mark 8³⁶). And if we consider this famous saying in its context, we shall see that what Jesus is warning men against is not what are commonly called 'sins' but the danger of a life wholly devoted to this world's values.

Now we may be sure that God, who is our Father, knows how we have to live in the world, that most of us have to work hard for our living, that we have responsibilities towards those whom we love and other legitimate duties which prevent us from escaping from the life of the world. It is probably true that God calls some people to separate themselves entirely from the world and devote themselves to prayer and meditation and good works of various kinds. But it is impossible to imagine that this is the Will of God for all men. Therefore we are bound to conclude that it is not only possible, but in a true sense the Will of God, that men should work hard in the affairs of this world, and yet maintain their spiritual life. This point is being stressed for the reason given above, that anyone actively engaged in the affairs of this world is bound to be tempted to think, not once but again and again, that the matters of the spirit are really a waste of time. The more deeply and intimately spiritual the matter is, the more irrelevant it will appear from the worldly point of view. So that while the worldly-minded man might give his assent to Church-going, might think prayer was a good idea for those whom it appeared to help, and might countenance a small dose of Bible-reading every day, yet he is likely to shy off such an intimacy with God as the Sacrament of Holy Communion as being so out of key with the rest of his living as to be meaningless.

Now we are all infected more than we sometimes realize by the prevailing atmosphere of thought around us. Therefore, if this Sacrament is to become to us a real part of our normal living, we shall almost certainly find that the chief part of our preparation is *preparation of the mind*. This does not necessarily mean desperate and strenuous effort, but it does mean a quiet and deliberate turning of the mind's eye from the transitory and unimportant to the important and eternal. We may naturally look with confidence for the help of God in this, for it is not His Purpose that we should be obsessed with the temporal, and the steady pressure of His Spirit is always drawing us to see and appreciate the spiritual. Yet, as in other spiritual matters, we shall find that the initiative, or at least the apparent initiative, must come from us. In plain terms, we have got to make a space when we can quietly think what we are doing in keeping this appointment.

Naturally every man must decide for himself how frequently he makes this special contact with God. It surely must never become merely a habit without conscious thought, nor on the other hand must it be so infrequent that its irradiating power upon ordinary living is dissipated long before it is renewed.

If this is an occasion when man can in a unique way make contact with his God and Saviour (and surely it must always be such an occasion, even when we ourselves are weary and depressed), there must be a certain deliberate preparation of body, mind, and soul. No one, of course, makes any social contact without taking the trouble to prepare; how much more ready should we be to prepare ourselves to meet God at these special points in our earthly pilgrimage? Let us consider our bodies first. Surely the best way of setting either mind or spirit free is to be as unaware of the body as possible. If the body is over-tired or out of sorts, it will be a drag upon the mind and spirit. We should be sensible enough to see that the body is in as good condition as possible, so that for the time being we may forget it.

Fasting before Communion is a custom of great antiquity, and many people find it a useful piece of self-discipline as well as aesthetically more appropriate to let this Holy Food be the first nourishment of the day to enter their bodies. But it must not be considered an *absolute essential*. For it has become such a fetish in some circles that those who break the rule of fasting are made to feel unnecessarily guilty, while those who fast for long periods not infrequently come to regard the fasting as at least as important as the Holy Food! At the same time there are numbers of unhappy souls whose early morning Communions are made miserable because of continual anxiety as to whether they are going to faint. To be brutally frank, it cannot really matter *physically* whether the Holy Bread and Wine enter an empty human stomach or whether within half an hour a hearty breakfast descends upon the sacred elements. Surely there is no point in so distressing the physical as to make the spiritual almost impossible of accomplishment. It is far more important for us to be able to forget about the body altogether, for what we are receiving is spiritual food and spiritual drink, even though it is under cover of a physical action.

Every man must obey his own conscience of course, but the healthy, hearty individual who is perfectly at ease for hours on an empty stomach must not impose his conscience upon a different physical type, to whom a small amount of food may make all the difference between physical self-forgetfulness and a miserable anxious pre-occupation.

Again, in posture we should aim at that position of the body which allows both relaxation and alertness of mind. No one would dream of attempting to tackle a difficult personal problem or even of solving a crossword puzzle while in a cramped and unnatural posture. Why should we expect the spirit to rise and worship and adore if the body is hideously uncomfortable?

We need also, as we have already said, to prepare the mind. Probably one of the greatest things that we can learn to do is to learn a holy relaxation. Sometimes we are unaware of the cause of our tensions, but often they are revealed to us as we deliberately open our mental life to the Spirit of God. We may find that we have been trying to preserve an inflated idea of ourselves; we may find that we have been childishly nursing a grudge against life or against someone else. There are innumerable causes of tension, but in the presence of perfect understanding they can be relaxed. We may need to apologize to

God or to other people, we may need an honest laugh at our pretentious selves, or we may need quite simply to hand responsibility, too big for ourselves, into the hand of God. To remove these tensions, possibly with the help of a trusted friend, is one of the essentials of preparation.

Having eased the mind of its strains, most of us need some central thought by which we can focus our attention during the time of Holy Communion. Obviously there are innumerable lines of thought which we may profitably follow. Here we suggest only a few.

(1) We may let our mind range quite freely over the vastness and complexity of God's wisdom and power, slowly allowing ourselves to realize that such a God focused Himself in the historic Person of Christ. From this point we let our minds dwell on the fact that Christ instituted this particular Sacrament; that though He is all about us, and indeed within us, yet it was no 'bright idea' of mankind but Christ's own purpose that He should give Himself to us in the mystery of the holy Bread and Wine.

(2) Sometimes we may think of the vast unseen world existing quite independently of the time-and-space set-up. We may think of the times when spiritual reality touches us very closely. We may use our imaginations freely, and not feel in the least ashamed that 'we that are in this tabernacle do groan being burdened'. We may remind ourselves that though we are citizens of the heavenly country, yet for the most part we walk by faith and not by sight. Our moments of illumination are few, yet here, so to

speak, is a guaranteed point where the eternal reaches through and touches the temporal. This Sacrament is a pledge from generation to generation, not only of the Love of God but of the everlasting nearness of the spiritual in the material.

(3) Sometimes we may think of ourselves, small and feeble as we are, carrying out, in company with millions of others, the Will of God in a world disrupted and disorganized. We think of ourselves together as representing Christ, however imperfectly, to a world desperately in need of the very qualities which He can provide. We think of our own deep need for the strength and vitality needed to represent Christ in our particular circle. We need the nourishment of Christ within, His very Personality potent and operative within our personalities. Then we think of what this Sacrament provides—the very nourishment, the very Presence we need, ready to be absorbed into our own selves.

(4) Sometimes we may think of the memorial aspect of the Great Sacrifice. We may have been guilty, as so many are, of allowing our own sense of sinfulness, or our own limited ideas of justice to caricature our idea of God. We may see Him again 'advertised' in this Sacrament as infinitely patient, vulnerable Love. The particular Communion we are attending is one end of a thread which leads back over the centuries unbroken to the Cross of Christ. 'God was in Christ reconciling the world unto Himself.' We may long reflect upon God's almost fantastic generosity in making reconciliation by this personal action and at this personal cost. Have we

by any chance been trying to worship the wrong kind of God?

(5) Sometimes we may reflect upon the nature of sacrifice. How often no lasting good is achieved without considerable cost to someone. We think of the lives of truly great men and women and how their great deeds have not influenced the lives of others without sacrifice. There is no need to be morbid, for often the sacrifices were cheerfully made. But it seems to be a principle of life that the lower must be denied to gain the higher, that no situation or person is redeemed without cost. Naturally we think of the One Great Sacrifice, now represented for us in poignant symbols in the broken bread and poured-out wine. We are to receive these things, this very Person, not only for our comfort and inspiration, but that we too may share, in a minor way no doubt, in the whole vast work of costly redemption. In our receiving of the sacrificial food there lies not only a deliberate allying of ourselves with the work of Christ, but an acceptance of the strength and joy to make whatever sacrifices come our way with courage and good humour.

These five suggestions are but a few of the ways in which we can deliberately turn our minds from the normal pre-occupation with earthly activities and become receptive to the Eternal Purpose.

FOURTEEN

PREPARATION—THE SOUL

LET us now consider that inmost sanctuary of our being which we may call the soul. We are not being psychological or meticulously logical here, and in any case the life of the mind and the life of the inmost soul overlap very considerably. But just as we are individual souls, different one from another, so surely is there a central core in the personality of each one of us, which is ours and ours alone. In this central citadel lie the springs of decision, and much as a tiny gland may affect the whole functioning of the body, so what goes on in this innermost soul will affect the whole attitude and activity of a man's life. Only God has access to this inmost soul, and He through His chivalry only by our permission.

But most of us, if we come to Communion at all, desire to give that permission. We want to be touched by God. We know only too well that we are soiled and weary, infected by the world around us far more than we care to be, and we want to be touched afresh with the never-failing Spring of Life Himself. How then can we prepare our souls?

(1) Without morbid 'muck-raking' we can freely admit our prides and cowardices, our lack of charity and the poor quality of our faith. Then we can accept the cordial of God's free forgiveness and reinstate-

ment. There is no question of our deserving such generous love, but it is a fact of life of which we can be quite sure. Then, if we have first relaxed the mind, we can allow our inmost selves to be both teachable and flexible. It is the hardest thing in the world for some people to admit that they have been wrong. But we really shall not get far in our spiritual life if, in the presence of Infinite Wisdom, we insist on being always right! God is the only one who is always right, and His ways, though firm, are much gentler than we may suppose.

(2) Then, without whipping ourselves up into a false state of emotion, let us be expectant. What the Bible calls 'faith' appears to be the essential link between the boundless resources of God and our own feebleness. The life of God within us is limited far more often than we know because we do not really believe in how much becomes possible through faith in God. 'Faith' is often like a faculty which has grown atrophied through disuse. It is that function of ours with which we can touch and hold the love and power of God.

(3) Lastly, we can gently train our souls to respond to the Love of God. We cannot force our own souls to love or to be grateful towards God any more than we can force anybody else to feel love or gratitude towards us. But we can at least put ourselves in the way of responding to God's Love. We can meditate upon it, upon the Nature and Character of God as revealed by Christ, and we can deliberately associate in our minds with God all those lovely

and heart-warming things which, despite the evil, adorn our common life. It is only love that can beget love, and self-giving that can stimulate self-giving. We cannot force the pace here but we can quietly look upon what sort of a Person our God really is.

Now it is obviously impossible for most people who live busy lives to make an elaborate preparation for Holy Communion, however desirable that may be. But if there is no preparation of mind and soul, what should be a tryst with God will in most cases degenerate into a 'duty attendance'. Of course, if we imagine that Holy Communion is some kind of magical prescription which can be received in regular doses to maintain spiritual health, preparation would hardly be necessary. But because it is no such thing, because it is the using of our highest faculties and the possible touching of our deepest springs of feeling, there must be at least a simple preparation of mind and soul. There will be times, naturally, when through ill-health or fatigue or that deadness of spirit which assails us all from time to time, there will be little emotional content. But this need not matter provided that in all honesty and sincerity of purpose we have confidently kept our appointment with God.

The Sacrament itself will vary in its emphasis according to different needs or tempers or circumstances. Sometimes it may be a tonic, sometimes it may be an inestimable refreshment, sometimes a revitalizing of the very springs of spiritual life, sometimes a glimpse of Heaven and an unspeakable joy, sometimes a renewal of dedication in deepest fellowship and with the Unseen Presence, but always it will be to those who love and believe an APPOINTMENT WITH GOD.

ENVOI

IT is a singularly unpleasant thought that a book
about Holy Communion is more likely to produce disagreement and controversy than one written on almost any other Christian subject. It seems a truly
terrible thing that this Sacred Appointment, which
was surely meant to unite, in actual practice divides
Christians more sharply than any other part of their
worship. Christians of various denominations may,
and frequently do, work together on social projects,
they may study the Scriptures together, and they may,
with the exception of the Roman Catholics, pray
together. But the moment attendance at the Lord's
Table is suggested up go the denominational barriers.

Whatever our tradition or point of view may be,
this denominational exclusiveness cannot surely be
the Will of God. If I, an Anglican Vicar, deny my
Free Church brother access to the Lord's Table set
up in my Church, what am I in fact suggesting? Do
I really mean that he is in some way a defective
Christian, so defective that I must not allow him to
approach our common Lord through the Anglican
rite? And if I were to think, as some appear to think,
that the Sacrament is only valid in my own Church,
am I condemning him to life-long participation in a
Mystery permanently deficient and ineffectual be-

cause the elements are not consecrated in the right way by the right kind of person?

Holy Communion is intended surely for all those who love our Lord and Saviour in sincerity and truth. This Mystery cannot be 'cornered' by any denomination and reserved exclusively for the use of its own members. We are one in Christ, whether we like it or not, and whether we approve of the other denominational tradition or not. Unless we are prepared to say that those nurtured in a different branch of the Christian Church are not Christians at all, I, for one, cannot see by what right I exclude my fellow-Christian from Communion with our common Lord.

Of course, when one talks like this, one is always accused of over-simplifying the issue, and disregarding the long and often bitter controversy which lies behind our divergent traditions. But must we for ever delve back into the past? Is it not conceivable that the Spirit of God could short-circuit our precious traditions and draw all Christians together in this central Act of worship? For it is to be noted that a good many of our differences are perpetuated, either consciously or unconsciously, by indoctrination. People do not very often change their demonination, and for the most part people remain in the denomination in which they were born and nurtured.

Those of us who have had the privilege of working among young people with little or no Christian background will know just how painful it is to choose a denomination for them. For many modern young people who are outside the Churches altogether neither know nor care about the differences between the various Churches, precious as those different traditions very often are to the older generation. But when, through the proclaiming of the Gospel, these young people become whole-heartedly converted to Christ and naturally wish to join a Christian fellowship, we have the heart-rending task of telling them just how divided the Churches are. These young ex-pagans find that being a Christian is not merely a matter of a changed life and devotion to the living Christ, but must include learning the point of view and special tenets of the denomination into which we direct them. Thus are the divisions perpetuated, God forgive us!

For what it is worth, I would make a strong plea that we do not exclude from the Lord's Table in our Church those who are undoubtedly sincere Christians. I cannot believe that to communicate together with our Lord should be regarded as the consummation, the final pinnacle, of the whole vast work of Reunion. Suppose it is the means and not the end. We might feel far more sharply the sin of our divisions and of our exclusiveness if we came humbly together to receive the Body and Blood of our Lord, and in that reception we might find such a quickening of our common devotion to Him that the divisions between us might be found not nearly so insuperable as we supposed.